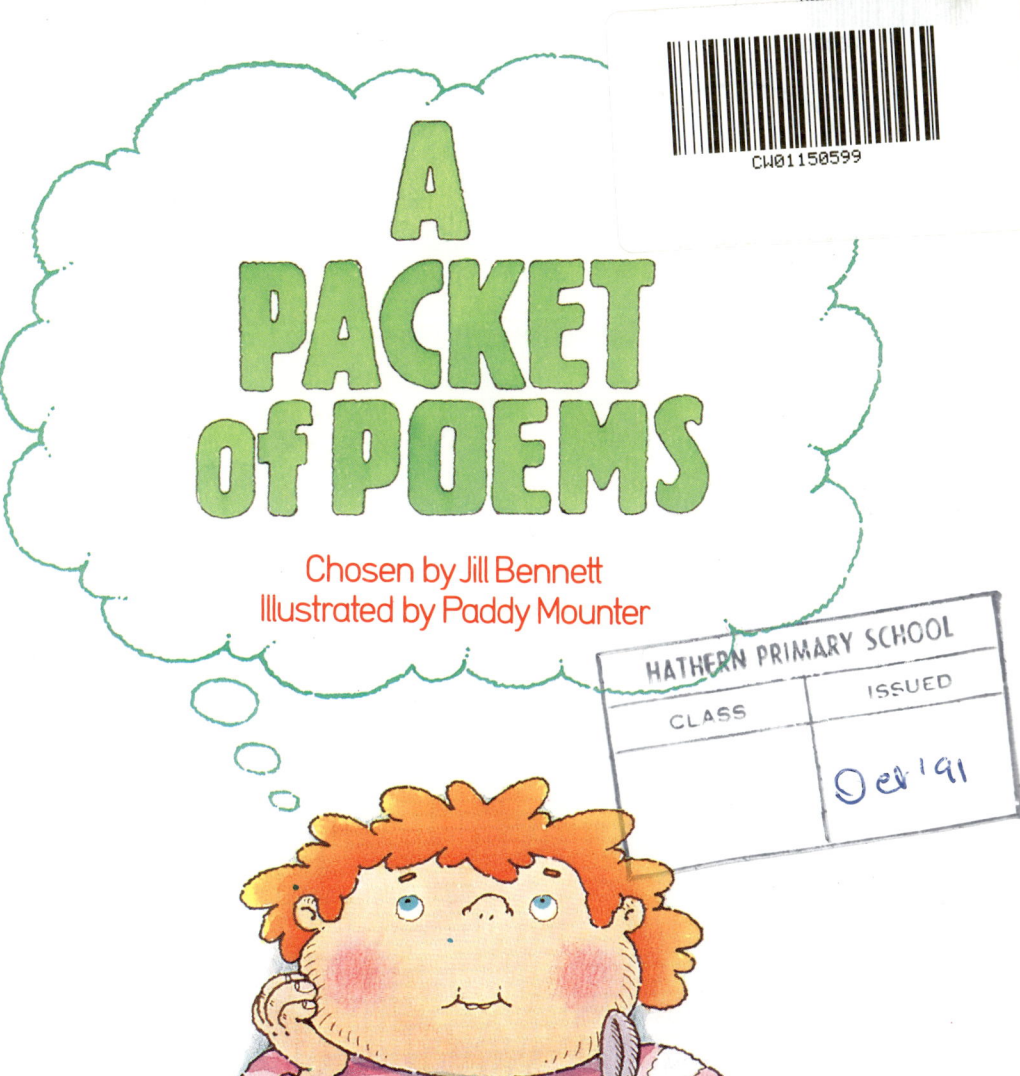

Oxford University Press, Walton Street, Oxford OX2 6DP

Oxford New York Toronto
Delhi Bombay Calcutta Madras Karachi
Petaling Jaya Singapore Hong Kong Tokyo
Nairobi Dar es Salaam Cape Town
Melbourne Auckland

and associated companies in
Berlin Ibadan

Oxford is a trade mark of Oxford University Press

Selection, arrangement and editorial matter
© Oxford University Press 1982

First published 1982
Reprinted 1984 (twice), 1986, 1987, 1989 (twice), 1991
First published in paperback 1986
Reprinted 1987, 1988, 1989 (twice), 1991

British Library Cataloguing in Publication Data

A packet of poems.
   1. Food-Poetry   2. English poetry
   I. Bennett, Jill
821'.008'0355
ISBN 0-19-276049-1

   1. Children's Poetry, English
   I. Bennett, Jill   II. Mounter, Paddy
821'.912'0809282   PZ8.3
ISBN 0-19-276066-1

For Sarah and Simon

Phototypeset by Tradespools Limited, Frome, Somerset

Printed in Hong Kong

CONTENTS

Supermarket	5
A Matter of Taste	19
Special Today	35
Mealtimes	49
Snacks	65
Hot Pot	81
Animal fare	91
Leftovers	99
Acknowledgements	
Index of Titles and First Lines	

Supermarket

I'm
lost
among a
maze of cans,
behind a pyramid
of jams, quite near
asparagus and rice,
close to the Oriental spice,
and just before sardines.
I hear my mother calling, 'Joe.
Where are you, Joe? Where did you
Go?' And I reply in voice concealed among
the candied orange peel, and packs of Chocolate Dreams.

'I
hear
you, Mother
dear, I'm here—
quite near the ginger ale
and beer, and lost among a

maze
of cans
behind a
pyramid of jams,
quite near asparagus
and rice, close to the
Oriental spice, and just before sardines.'

But
still
my mother
calls me, 'Joe!
Where are you, Joe?
Where did you go?'

'Somewhere
around asparagus
that's in a sort of
        broken glass,
             beside a kind of m-
                      ess-
                            y jell
that's near a tower of cans that f
                                    e
                                 l
                                 l
and squashed the Chocolate Dreams.'

Felice Holman

Cries of London

Cherries

Here's round and sound,
Black and white heart cherries,
Two-pence a pound.

Hot Cross Buns

Hot cross buns, hot cross buns,
One a penny, two a penny, hot cross buns.
If you have no daughters, give them to your sons,
One a penny, two a penny, hot cross buns.

Oranges

    Here's oranges nice!
    At a very small price,
I sell them all two for a penny.
    Ripe, juicy, and sweet,
    Just fit to eat,
So customers buy a good many.

Apples

Here are fine golden pippins,
Who'll buy them, who'll buy?
Nobody in London sells better than I,
Who'll buy them, who'll buy?

Pears

Pears for pies,
Come feast your eyes!
Ripest pears
Of every size.
    Who'll buy?
    Who'll buy?

Milk below

Rain, frost or snow, hot or cold,
    I travel up and down,
The cream and milk you buy of me
    Is the best in all the town.
For custards, puddings, or for tea,
    There's none like those you buy of me.

anon

The peanut seller

Peanuts!
Two bags for five!

They brush your teeth,
They curl your hair;
They make you feel
Like a millionaire!

Peanuts!
Two bags for five!

Street-cry from New Orleans

V is for Vegetables

The country vegetables scorn
   To lie about in shops,
They stand upright as they were born
   In neatly-patterned crops;

And when you want your dinner you
   Don't buy it from a shelf,
You find a lettuce fresh with dew
   And pull it for yourself;

You pick an apronful of peas
   And shell them on the spot,
You cut a cabbage, if you please,
   To pop into the pot.

Eleanor Farjeon

The Cupboard

I know a little cupboard,
With a teeny tiny key,
And there's a jar of Lollipops
    For me, me, me.

It has a little shelf, my dear,
As dark as dark can be,
And there's a dish of Banbury Cakes
    For me, me, me.

I have a small fat grandmamma,
With a very slippery knee,
And she's Keeper of the Cupboard,
    With the key, key, key.

And when I'm very good, my dear,
As good as good can be,
There's Banbury Cakes, and Lollipops
    For me, me, me.

Walter de la Mare

Obsequious Prawn

Obsequious Prawn
Was very forlorn
And didn't know what to do.

His reason to fret—
He'd been caught in a net
And was heading for somebody's stew.

Michael Dugan

July

In July
I'll take a peep
into the cool
and fishy deep
where chicken soup
is selling cheap.
Selling once
selling twice
selling chicken soup
with rice.

Maurice Sendak

The Outlaw

Into the house of a Mrs MacGruder
Came a very big outlaw
With a real six-shooter,
And he kicked the door
With his cowboy boot
And he searched the place
For valuable loot,
And he didn't take off his cowboy hat
But he quickly unlimbered his cowboy gat
And he cocked the gun
And he took his aim
And he called that Mrs MacG by name
And he said in a terrible outlaw drawl,
'Git me that cake... and git it all!'

And Mrs MacGruder patted his head,
'You may have a slice with some milk,' she said.

Felice Holman

Taffy was a Welshman

Taffy was a Welshman,
    Taffy was a thief,
Taffy came to my house
    And stole a piece of beef.

I went to Taffy's house,
    Taffy wasn't in,
I jumped upon his Sunday hat
    And poked it with a pin.

Taffy was a Welshman,
    Taffy was a sham,
Taffy came to my house
    And stole a leg of lamb.

I went to Taffy's house,
    Taffy was not there,
I hung his coat and trousers
    To roast before a fire.

Taffy was a Welshman,
    Taffy was a cheat,
Taffy came to my house
    And stole a piece of meat.

I went to Taffy's house,
    Taffy wasn't home;
Taffy came to my house
    And stole a marrow bone.

anon.

The King's Breakfast

The King asked
The Queen, and
The Queen asked
The Dairymaid:
'Could we have some butter for
The Royal slice of bread?'
The Queen asked
The Dairymaid,
The Dairymaid
Said, 'Certainly,
I'll go and tell
The cow
Now
Before she goes to bed.'

The Dairymaid
She curtsied,
And went and told
The Alderney:
'Don't forget the butter for
The Royal slice of bread.'
The Alderney
Said sleepily:
'You'd better tell
His Majesty
That many people nowadays
Like marmalade Instead.'

The Dairymaid
Said, 'Fancy!'
And went to
Her Majesty.
She curtsied to the Queen, and
She turned a little red:

'Excuse me
Your Majesty,
For taking of
The liberty,
But marmalade is tasty, if
It's very
Thickly
Spread.'

The Queen said
'Oh!'
And went to
His Majesty:
'Talking of the butter for
The royal slice of bread,
Many people
Think that
Marmalade
Is nicer.
Would you like to try a little
Marmalade
Instead?'

The King said,
'Bother!'
And then he said,
'Oh, deary me!'
The King sobbed, 'Oh deary me!'
And went back to bed.
'Nobody,'
He whimpered,
'Could call me
A fussy man;
I *only* want
A little bit
Of butter for
My bread!'

15

The Queen said
'There, there!'
And went to
The Dairymaid.
The Dairymaid
Said, 'There, there!'
And went to the shed.
The cow said
There, there!
'I didn't really
Mean it;
Here's milk for his porringer
And butter for his bread.'

The Queen took
The butter
And brought it to
His Majesty;
The King said,
'Butter, eh?'
And bounced out of bed.
'Nobody,' he said,
As he kissed her
Tenderly,
'Nobody,' he said,
As he slid down
The banisters,
'Nobody,
My darling,
Could call me
A fussy man—
BUT
I do like a little bit of butter to my bread!'

A. A. Milne

The fate of the Supermarket manager

There once was a Supermarket manager
And a very happy manager was he.

He *reduced the prices*
Of the lollies and the ices!
He made *huge cuts*
On the fruit and nuts!
Corn-flakes, steaks
And home-bake cakes,
Dog-food, detergent,
Devil-fish, dates,
He sold at *half*
The market rates!
And (so my sister
Said to me)
He put stickers
On the knickers
In the Lingerie
Saying:
Prices down
By 15p!
And he wrote, as a treat,
By the luncheon meat:
YOU'D HAVE TO BE BARMY
TO BUY THIS SALAMI
So he gave it away
For free!

Yes, there once was a Supermarket manager
And a very happy manager was he.

What a bloke!

He was much admired.

The shop went broke.

He was fired.

Kit Wright

A matter of taste

What does your tongue like the most?
Chewy meat or crunchy toast?

A lumpy bumpy pickle or tickly pop?
A soft marshmallow or a hard lime drop?

Hot pancakes or a sherbet freeze?
Celery noise or quiet cheese?

Or do you like pizza
More than any of these?

Eve Merriam

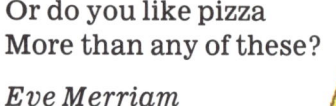

A fisherman living in Deal

A fisherman living in Deal,
When asked what he liked for a meal,
Said, 'All kinds of fish,
But my favourite dish
Is a properly stuffed jellied eel.'

Charles Connell

Isabel Jones & Curabel Lee

Isabel Jones & Curabel Lee
Lived on butter and bread and tea,
And as to that they would both agree:
Isabel, Curabel, Jones & Lee.

Isabel said: While prunes have stones
They aren't a promising food for Jones;
Curabel said: Well, as for me,
Tripe is a terrible thing for Lee.

There's not a dish of fowl or fish
For which we wish, said I. & C.
And that is why until we die
We'll eat no pie, nor beg nor buy
But butter and bread and a trace of tea.
(Signed) *Isabel Jones & Curabel Lee.*

David McCord

Karen doesn't like a cone

Karen doesn't like a cone
Unless there's ice cream in it.
She knows just how to eat it then:
She licks
And licks,
Then spins it.

But when she talks
She lets it drip
And just forgets to spin it,
And then she is a pretty mess
In just about a minute.

Arnold Spilka

Chicken & chips

Here are some of our favourite foods
and we like them all with chips:

Chicken and chips,
Chicken and chips,
Everyone here likes chicken and chips.
    We eat them all day
      Never throw them away
We all like chicken and chips.

Choc ice and chips,
Choc ice and chips,
Everyone here likes choc ice and chips.
    We eat them all day
      Never throw them away
We all like choc ice and chips.

Chop suey and chips,
Chop suey and chips,
Everyone here likes chop suey and chips.
    We eat them all day
      Never throw them away
We all like chop suey and chips.

Chips and chips,
Chips and chips,
Everyone here likes chips and chips,
    We eat them all day
      Never throw them away
We all like chips and chips.

anon.

Giants' delight

Vats of soup
On table trays
Side of shark
With mayonnaise
Haunch of ox
With piles of mice
Mounds of gristle
Served on ice
Bone of mammoth
Head of boar
Whales and serpents
By the score
Tons of cole slaw
Stacks of rabbits
(Giants have such
Piggy habits)
Then, at last,
There comes a stew
Full of buffalo
And ewe
Followed by
Some chocolate cakes
Big enough
For stomachaches

Steven Kroll

Be nice to rhubarb

Please say a word for rhubarb,
    It hasn't many chums
For people like banana splits
    Or fancy juicy plums.

They slice the sweet, sweet melon
    Or gather tasty pears,
But if you mention rhubarb pie
You get the *rhu*dest stares.

They praise the yellow lemon,
    The golden orange cool,
But rhubarb's never mentioned
    —Or that's the general *rhu*le.

For rhubarb stewed and blushing
    I've only this to say,
If they should cast an unkind barb
    I'll see they *rhu* the day.

Max Fatchen

Say Cheese

At Christmas the STILTON
Was spilt on the Wilton,
The rare CAMEMBERT
Was as fine as can be,
But at New Year the GRUYERE
It just went straight through yer,
The CHEDDAR was bedder
But as for the BRIE,
Aaaaaaaagh! And the PORT SALUD!
Swallow one morsel, you
Kept to your bed
For a week and a day,
And if you tried WENSLEYDALE
You quite *immensely'd* ail,
Hospital-bound
Till they wheeled you away!

No better was EMMENTHAL,
Sour and inclement, all
Cratered and pocked
Like a view of the moon!
And while some are crazy
For creamed BEL PAESE,
Myself, I'd eat forcemeat
Or horsemeat as soon!

The LEICESTER was best o'
The bunch, but the rest o'
Them curled up your stomach.
Though GLOUCESTER (times two)
And jaundiced old CHESHIRE
I'd taste under pressure,
Nothing would get me,
No nothing would get me,
But nothing would get me
To try DANISH BLUE!

Kit Wright

Bananas and cream

Bananas and cream,
Bananas and cream:
All we could say was
Bananas and cream.

We couldn't say fruit,
We wouldn't say cow,
We didn't say sugar—
We don't say it now.

Bananas and cream,
Bananas and cream,
All we could shout was
Bananas and cream.

We didn't say why,
We didn't say how;
We forgot it was fruit,
We forgot the old cow;
We *never* said sugar,
We only said WOW!

Bananas and cream,
Bananas and cream;
All that we want is
Bananas and cream!

We didn't say dish,
We didn't say spoon;
We said not tomorrow,
But NOW and HOW SOON.

Bananas and cream,
Bananas and cream?
We yelled for bananas,
Bananas and scream!

David McCord

O Sliver of Liver

O sliver of liver,
Get lost! Go away!
You tremble and quiver
O sliver of liver—
You set me a-shiver
And spoil my day—
O sliver of liver,
Get lost! Go away!

Myra Cohn Livingston

Peculiar

I once knew a boy who was odd as could be:
He liked to eat cauliflower and broccoli
And spinach and turnips and rhubarb pies
And he didn't like hamburgers or French fries.

Eve Merriam

The Parsnip

The parsnip, children, I repeat
Is simply an anaemic beet.
Some people call the parsnip edible;
Myself, I find this claim incredible.

Ogden Nash

The Meal

Timothy Tompkins had turnips and tea.
The turnips were tiny.
He ate at least three.
And then, for dessert,
He had onions and ice.
He liked that so much
That he ordered it twice.
He had two cups of ketchup,
A prune, and a pickle.
'Delicious,' said Timothy.
'Well worth a nickel.'
He folded his napkin
And hastened to add,
'It's one of the loveliest breakfasts I've had.'

Karla Kuskin

The Pizza

Look at itsy-bitsy Mitzi!
See her figure slim and ritzy!
She eatsa
Pizza!
Greedy Mitzi!
She no longer itsy-bitsy!

Ogden Nash

Dilly Dilly Piccalilli

Dilly Dilly Piccalilli
Tell me something very silly:
There was a chap his name was Bert
He ate the buttons off his shirt.

Clyde Watson

Cucumbers vs pickles

Cucumbers always give me squirms:
With them I've *never* come to terms.
But pickles, on the other hand,
The bitter, sweet, the mild, the bland:
Dills, gherkins, fat ones, thin green worms—
Delicious! Do you understand?

David McCord

My uncle roasted a Kangaroo

My uncle roasted a kangaroo,
Gave me the grizzelly end to chew!
Was that a very nice thing to do,
To give me the grizzelly end
    to chew,
        to chew,
            to chew, to chew, to chew?

William Cole

Thanks anyhow

When I was a boy in your town
    I lived on wax and cheese.
I got the cheese from a billy goat.
    I got the wax from bees.

Dinner with a billy goat.
    Breakfast with the bees.
What's for lunch—Banana peel.
    But first you must say please.

Dinner was bad and breakfast worse.
    Lunch was, alas, a mess.
I tried the food at your house.
    I liked it even less!

Dinner with a bunch of brats.
    Breakfast at the zoo.
Never mind lunch—I'd rather munch
    Cardboard than eat with you.

John Ciardi

A blackberry picker called Sam

A blackberry picker called Sam
Ate berries where others ate ham.
    A doctor, who pried,
      Said, 'Sir, your inside
Would make most delectable jam.'

Max Fatchen

Beautiful Soup

Beautiful Soup, so rich and green,
Waiting in a hot tureen!
Who for such dainties would not stoop?
Soup of the evening, beautiful Soup!

Soup of the evening, beautiful Soup!
    Beau-ootiful Soo-oop!
    Beau-ootiful Soo-oop!
Soo-oop of the e-e-evening,
    Beautiful, beautiful Soup!

Beautiful Soup! Who cares for fish,
Game, or any other dish?
Who would not give all else for two
Pennyworth only of beautiful Soup?
Pennyworth only of beautiful Soup?
    Beau-ootiful Soo-oop!
    Beau-ootiful Soo-oop!
Soo-oop of the e-e-evening,
    Beautiful, beauti-FUL SOUP!

Lewis Carroll

Pumberly Pott's unpredictable niece

Pumberly Pott's unpredictable niece
declared with her usual zeal
that she would devour, by piece after piece,
her uncle's new automobile.

She set to her task very early one morn
by consuming the whole carburettor;
then she swallowed the windshield, the headlights and horn,
and the steering wheel just a bit later.

She chomped on the doors, on the handles and locks,
on the valves and the pistons and rings;
on the air pump and fuel pump and spark plugs and shocks,
on the brakes and the axles and springs.

When her uncle arrived she was chewing a hash
made of leftover hoses and wires
(she'd just finished eating the clutch and the dash
and the steel-belted radial tyres).

'Oh what have you done to my auto,' he cried,
'you strange unpredictable lass?'
'The thing wouldn't work, Uncle Pott,' she replied,
and he wept, 'It was just out of gas.'

Jack Prelutsky

Special Today

i
We can recommend our soups
And offer thick or thin.
One is known as *Packet*
The other known as *Tin*.

ii
The flying-fish makes a very fine dish;
As good as plaice or skate
When sizzled in fat; but be certain that
You tether it to your plate.

iii
Now this hot-dog makes an excellent snack;
Our sausages are best pork.
If you can't get it down, please don't send it back,
But take it for a nice brisk walk.

iv
Are you tempted by our fried fish-fingers?
The last customer to succumb
Was hard to please; he demanded
Why we couldn't provide a fish thumb.

v
Bubble-and-squeak is splendid stuff
And Chef takes endless trouble
But if you feel you'd like a change
Then try our squeak-and-bubble.

vi
Try our cabinet pudding
Or a slice of home-made cake;
We serve with each, quite free of charge,
A pill for your tummy-ache.

Vernon Scannell

Gretchen in the kitchen

I see you're here to sneak some looks
at Gretchen and the way she cooks.
So peek through Gretchen's kitchen door
and watch what Gretchen has in store.

I do believe I'll boil a brew,
a wretchedly repulsive stew,
that only Gretchen can prepare.
Stop shaking! It's all right to stare.

I start with quarts of curdled mud,
and stir in spoons of dragon's blood,
then add one nose of nasty newt,
one rubber glove, one leather boot.

Then deep into my reeking vat
I toss a tongue of pickled rat,
some salted spiders (half a pound),
two candied eyeballs, sweet and round.

A lizard's gizzard, lightly mashed,
an ogre's backbone, slightly smashed,
warts of toad and scales of fish
contribute body to the dish.

Serpents' teeth and tails of mice
supply a special sort of spice
and lastly, just a pinch of paste
to season things to Gretchen's taste.

My little mix is all fixed up.
Would someone care to try a cup?
Let's hear your answers ... yes or no
... now, where did everybody go?

Jack Prelutsky

Pimlico

Pimlico, pamlico, pumpkins and peas!
Pepper them properly , else you will sneeze,
Pop in a pipkin and leave them till one,
Pimlico, pamlico, then they'll be done!

Eleanor Farjeon

Lentils

Lentils, lentils,
Anyone seen the lentils?
They're in the pot
All sizzling hot;
They bubble away
For a year and a day;
They stew and stew
The whole time through,
And lentil soup
Is ready for you.

Groans, groans
Groans, groans
It's dry as bones
And hard as stones.

Brian Alderson (adapter)

A peanut

A peanut sat on the railroad track,
His heart was all a-flutter.
Along came a train, the 10.15—
Toot-toot! peanut butter!

anon.

A quick skip before dinner

Peepy pipey peppercorn,
Leaping like a leprechaun,
Jumped into an Irish stew,
And turned it into something new.

Cynthia Mitchell

Betty Botter's batter

Betty Botter bought some butter,
But, she said, the butter's bitter;
If I put it in my batter
It will make my batter bitter.
But a bit of better butter,
That would make my batter better.
So she bought a bit of butter
Better than her bitter butter,
And she put it in her batter
And the batter was not bitter.
So t'was better Betty Botter
Bought a bit of better butter.

anon.

King Arthur

When good King Arthur ruled this land,
    He was a goodly King;
He stole three pecks of barley-meal
    To make a bag-pudding.

A bag-pudding the King did make,
    And stuffed it well with plums,
And in it put great lumps of fat,
    As big as my two thumbs.

The King and Queen did eat thereof,
    And noblemen beside;
And what they could not eat that night,
    The Queen next morning fried.

anon.

UCKG!

Once I went to the fridge—
saw our jug in there
and I thought:
what's in it?
A syrup
what syrup?
smell it—smells nice
finger in—lick it—
tastes nice
lift the jug and drink a bit
this is good
this is peach syrup
what a drink!
so I drank the lot.

Not long after—a few days later—
I went to the fridge
saw our jug in there
what's in it?
A syrup
what syrup?
smell it
O yes this is the peach syrup again
lift the jug and drink some
drink some more, drink some more
drank the lot.

Not long after—a few days later
I went to the fridge
saw our jug in there
what's in it?
A syrup—yes!
here we go again
lift the jug and fill my mouth
with that thick sweet juice

Uckg!

this isn't peach
this is uckg.
my mouth is full of oil
thick cooking oil

I wonder
who put *that* there?

Michael Rosen

Catherine

Catherine said, 'I think I'll bake
A most delicious chocolate cake.'
She took some mud and mixed it up
While adding water from a cup
And then some weeds and nuts and bark
And special gravel from the park
A thistle and a dash of sand.
She beat out all the lumps by hand.
And on the top she wrote 'To You'
The way she says the bakers do
And then she signed it 'Fondly, C.'
And gave the whole of it to me.
I thanked her but I wouldn't dream
Of eating cake without ice cream.

Karla Kuskin

If you're no good at cooking

If you're no good at cooking,
Can't fry or bake,

Here's something you
Can always make. Take

Three very ordinary
Slices of bread:

Stack the second
On the first one's head.

Stack the third
On top of that.

There! Your three slices
Lying pat.

So what have you got?
A BREAD SANDWICH,

That's what!
Why not?

Kit Wright

Davy Dumpling

Davy Davy Dumpling,
   Boil him in the pot;
Sugar him and butter him,
   And eat him while he's hot.

anon.

Ruptured Recipes

Cinnamon and arrowroot,
Candy canes and rice,
Sago, flour and candied peel,
Crocodiles and mice,
Rice, mice, crocodiles,
Candied peel and flour,
Mix it with a feather
And boil for half an hour.

Take a dozen little boys
Put them through a sieve,
Stew them till they thicken
Ask them where they live,
Dot them with some butter
Label them with ink,
Spread the lot with mustard
To make a pleasant drink.

Beat together nuts and may,
Break an egg into the hole,
Shake in half a pound of salt
And stir till mixture leaves the bowl,
Catch and skin it quickly, then
Stuff it with a shovel,
Bake it in a maximum
And send it to the devil.

Fresh dandelions are best for this,
Pick them when they're green
To make a dish of buttered grubs
Fit to serve a queen.
Grate a brick until quite fine
Whip it up with jam,
Cover grubs with brickdust sauce
And serve on slices of ham.

To serve a tasty doormat
Bake it till it crumbles,
Offer it a cup of tea
Don't worry if it mumbles.
Coat it with a paste of tar,
Fry it till it's thinner,
Take care it doesn't smoke at all
And serve it up for dinner.

Barbara Giles

What's in the cupboard?

What's in the cupboard?
Says Mrs Hubbard.
A knuckle of veal,
Says Mrs Beal.
Is that all?
Says Mrs Ball.
And enough too,
Says Mrs Glue—

And away they all flew.

anon.

Witches' Menu

Live lizard, dead lizard
Marinated, fried.
Poached lizard, pickled lizard
Salty lizard hide.

Hot lizard, cold lizard
Lizard over ice.
Baked lizard, boiled lizard
Lizard served with spice.

Sweet lizard, sour lizard
Smoked lizard heart.
Leg of lizard, loin of lizard
Lizard a la carte.

Sonja Nikolay

Advice to young cooks

Before you start to cook
Your latest library book,
First read it without haste
To ensure you like the taste,
And when you've read it through
Then add it to your stew.

Michael Dugan

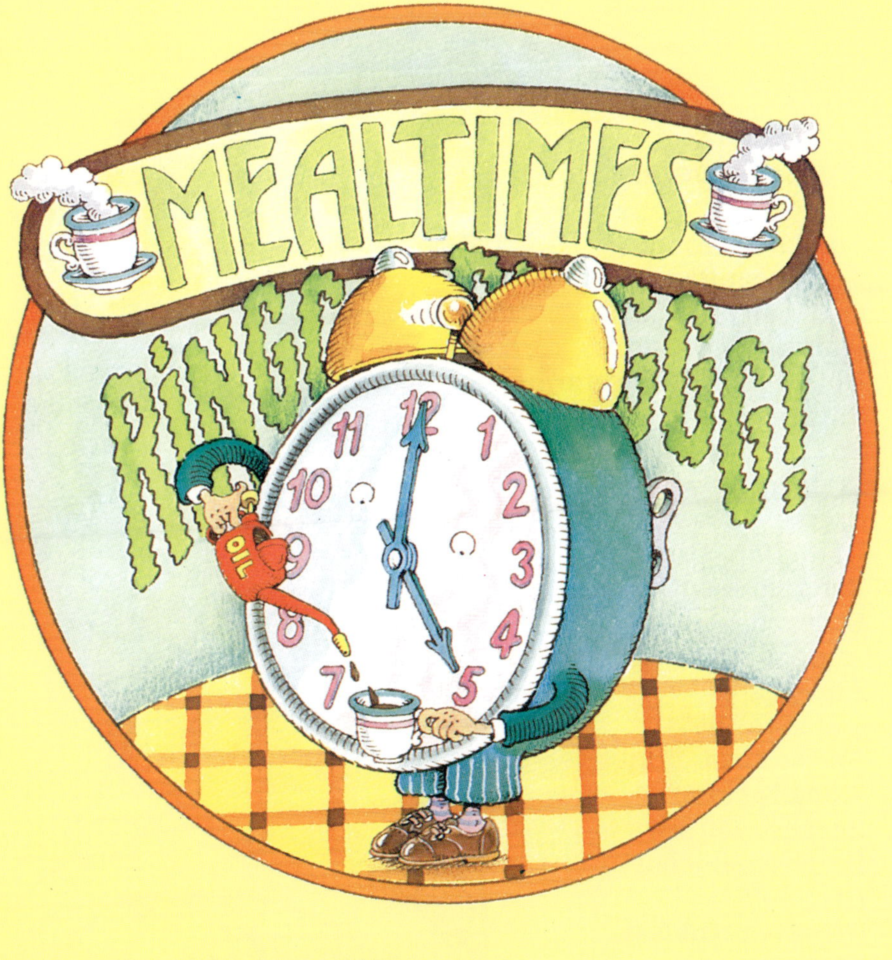
MEALTIMES
OIL

Through the Teeth

Through the teeth
And past the gums.
Look out, stomach,
Here it comes!

anon.

An Emergency

Sunday morning,
And I hear Papa snoring.
Oh it can be so boring
Waiting for breakfast,
But I daren't wake him, he
Says (except in an emergency).
So I pretend the snoring
Is just a lion roaring,
Starving for red meat
Or *anything* to eat,
Even oatmeal!
Even me!
And the roaring is nearer
And clearer
Out in the hall!
And so I call
'Papa!' at last,
Because you see
It's an emergency.
And *then*
We have breakfast.

Felice Holman

Breakfast

Is it coffee for breakfast?
I wish it was tea!
Is it jam? Oh, why can't there
Be honey for me?

Is it brown bread-and-butter?
I wish it was toast!
Is it just bread-and-milk?
I like porridge the most.

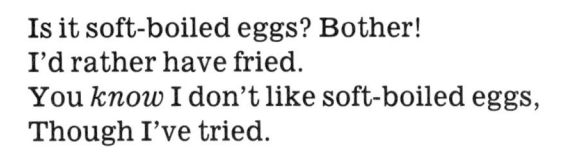

Is it soft-boiled eggs? Bother!
I'd rather have fried.
You *know* I don't like soft-boiled eggs,
Though I've tried.

Of all horrid breakfasts
This breakfast's the worst!—
Who tumbled out of his bed
Wrong leg first?

Eleanor Farjeon

There was a king

There was a king who had four sons,
For breakfast they had currant buns,
It seems a funny thing to me,
But every day they each ate three.
Every day the baker came,
Every day it was the same,
Every day at half past eight
He left twelve buns at the castle gate.

anon.

Zanzibar Pete and Zoom-along Dick

Zanzibar Pete and Zoom-along Dick
took a picnic to eat in the park.
They took so much food
(without being rude)
that they had to stay there until dark.

Zanzibar Pete and Zoom-along Dick
picked up all of the litter they'd made.
Then they felt so much thinner
they went home to dinner
and ate a lot more, I'm afraid.

Nancy Chambers

Jam

'Spread,' said Toast to Butter,
And Butter spread.
'That's better, Butter,'
Toast said.

'Jam,' said Butter to Toast.
'Where are you, Jam,
When we need you most?'
Jam: 'Here I am,

Strawberry, trickly and sweet.
How are you, Spoon?'
'I'm helping somebody eat,
I think, pretty soon.'

David McCord

School Dinners

If you stay to school dinners
Better throw them aside;
A lot of kids didn't,
A lot of kids died.
The meat is made of iron,
The spuds are made of steel;
If that don't get you
The afters will.

anon.

Baby's Drinking Song

   Sip a little
Sup a little
   From your little
Cup a little
   Sup a little
Sip a little
   Put it to your
Lip a little
   Tip a little
Tap a little
   Not into your
Lap or it'll
   Drip a little
Drop a little
   On the table
Top a little.

James Kirkup

The other day when I met Dick

The other day when I met Dick
He said, 'I think I'm feeling sick.
A little while back I was feeling fine
And eating my breakfast. I ate nine
Helpings of ham, and ten of fish,
And some of the meat on my Daddy's dish,
And a tub or two of the best wheat flakes,
And another tub of hot pancakes.
Then I ate a pan full of buns with jam,
And another helping or two of ham.

My, I felt fine!
         —But here I am,
Just a little bit later, and as you see,
As sick as a dog. What *can* it be?
I wish I knew what was doing it.
Do you think it would help if I ate a bit?'

John Ciardi

Mary had a little lamb

Mary had a little lamb,
She ate it with mint sauce,
And everywhere that Mary went
That lamb went too, of course!

anon.

Dave Dirt came to dinner

Dave Dirt came to dinner
    And he stuck his chewing gum
Underneath the table
    And it didn't please my Mum

And it didn't please my Granny
    Who was a sight to see
When she got up from the table
    With the gum stuck to her knee

Where she put her cup and saucer
    When she sat and drank her tea
And the saucer and the chewing gum
    Got stuck as stuck can be

And she staggered round the kitchen
    With a saucer on her skirt—
No, it didn't please my Granny
    But it
        PLEASED
        DAVE
           DIRT

Kit Wright

Dinner at Blunderbore's

The giant Blunderbore,
About to dine on pork,
Called in a blunderborian roar:
'Bring me my knife and fork!'

And in four servants ran,
Trotting for dear life:
At each end of the fork one man,
And two men to the knife.

'Goodness,' one captive cried,
'This giant's awfully big.
But I'd be still more terrified
To meet a giant's pig.'

Roy Fuller

Minnie

Minnie can't make her mind up,
Minnie can't make up her mind!
    They ask her at tea,
    'Well, what shall it be?'
    And Minnie says, 'Oh,
    Muffins, please! no,
    Sandwiches—yes,
    Please, egg-and-cress—
    I mean a jam one,
    Or is there a ham one,
Or is there another kind?
    Never mind!
                  Cake
    Is what I will take,
The sort with the citron-rind,
    Or p'r'haps the iced one—
    Or is there a spiced one,
Or is there the currant kind?'
    When tea is done
    She hasn't begun,
She's always the one behind,
Because she can't make her mind up,
Minnie *can't* make up her mind!

Eleanor Farjeon

The Giant

    Fee, fi, fo, fum,
    I smell the blood of an Englishman:
    Be he alive or be he dead,
    I'll grind his bones to make my bread.

    anon.

Give up slimming, Mum

My Mum
is short
and plump
and pretty
and I wish
she'd give up
slimming.

So does Dad.

Her cooking's
delicious—
you can't
beat it—
but you really can
hardly bear
to eat it—
the way she sits
with her eyes
brimming,
watching you
polish off
the spuds
and trimmings
while she
has nothing
herself but a small
thin dry
diet biscuit:
that's all.

My Mum
is short

and plump
and pretty
and I wish
she'd give up
slimming.

So does Dad.

She says she
looks as though
someone had
sat on her—
BUT WE LIKE MUM
WITH A BIT
OF FAT ON HER!

Kit Wright

Eating at the Restaurant of How Chow Now

Ever eaten Chinese food?
Eaten with chopsticks made of wood,
Holding one chopstick nice and tight?
The other never works just right.

Or if it does, the tight one teeters.
These wooden hinges aren't for eaters
Like you and me. We get a grip
On bamboo shoots, and off they slip!

Thin mushroom slices, peapods, rice,
Hockeypuck meat, need some device
to gather in and underslide them.
Forks are good. But Chinese hide them.

Same with knives: *they can't abide them!*

David McCord

Little Miss Muffet

Little Miss Muffet,
Sat on a tuffet,
Eating her Irish stew.
Along came a spider
And sat down beside her,
So she ate *him* up, too.

Little Miss Muffet sat on a tuffet,
Eating her curds and whey.
Along came a spider who sat down beside her
And said, 'Whatcha got in the bowl, sweetheart?'

Little Miss Muffet sat on a tuffet,
Eating her curds and whey.
Along came a spider who sat down beside her
And said, 'Is this seat taken?'

anon.

The Picnic

We brought a rug for sitting on,
Our lunch was in a box.
The sand was warm. We didn't wear
Hats or Shoes or Socks.

Waves came curling up the beach.
We waded. It was fun.
Our sandwiches were different kinds.
I dropped my jelly one.

Dorothy Aldis

I met a man that showed me a trick

I met a man that showed me a trick.
He said to me, 'My name is NICK,
Or PETE, or SAM. You may take your pick.'

'Well, then,' I said to him, 'I'll pick NICK.'

So he took out a box and gave me some bread,
And milk, and jam, and when I had fed,
He picked up the box and sighed and said,
'Good-bye, I'm going home to bed.'

And off he went. (If you guessed the trick,
This is the way you can always trick NICK.
And when you do, you'll have a PICNIC.)

John Ciardi

One summer at tea

There was a young parson named Perkins,
Exceedingly fond of small gherkins.
    One summer at tea
    He ate forty-three,
Which pickled his internal workin's.

anon.

Salt, Mustard, Vinegar, Pepper

Salt, Mustard, Vinegar, Pepper,
French almond rock,
Bread and butter for your supper
That's all mother's got.
Fish and chips and coca cola,
Put them in a pan,
Irish stew and ice cream soda,
We'll eat all we can.

Salt, Mustard, Vinegar, Pepper,
French almond rock,
Bread and butter for your supper
That's all mother's got.
Eggs and bacon, salted herring,
Put them in a pot,
Pickled onions, apple pudding,
We will eat the lot.

Salt, Mustard, Vinegar, Pepper,
Pig's head and trout,
Bread and butter for your supper
O-U-T spells out.

Traditional English

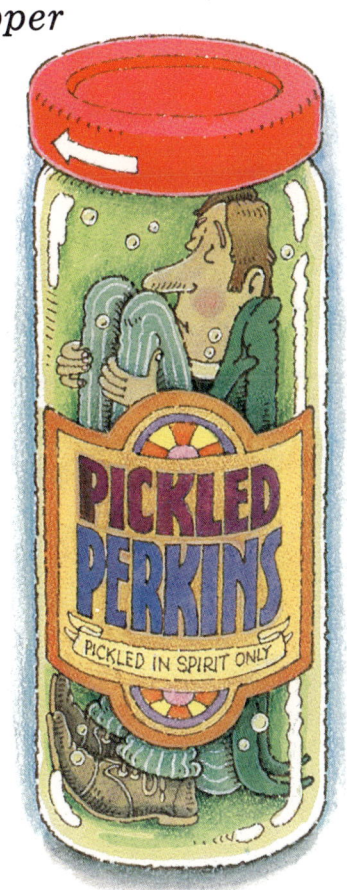

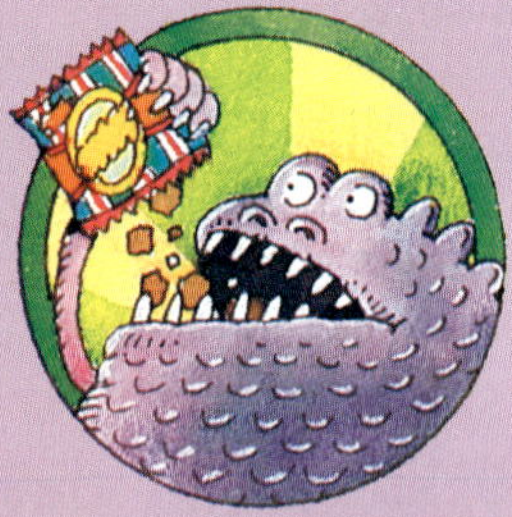

MONSTER PACK
Snacks
ASSORTED NASTIES
MONSTERSODIUMGOULTOMATE
FLAVOUR

Herbert Glerbett

Herbert Glerbett, rather round,
swallowed sherbet by the pound,
fifty pounds of lemon sherbet
went inside of Herbert Glerbett.

With that glop inside his lap
Herbert Glerbett took a nap,
and as he slept, the boy dissolved,
and from the mess a thing evolved—

a thing that is a ghastly green,
a thing the world had never seen,
a puddle thing, a gooey pile
of something strange that does not smile.

Now if you're wise, and if you're sly,
you'll swiftly pass this creature by,
it is no longer Herbert Glerbett.
Whatever it is, do not disturb it.

Jack Prelutsky

The Glutton

Oh Molly, Molly, Molly
I've eaten too much pie
I've eaten too much custard
I think I'm going to die!

Just one more plate of jelly
Before I pass away
Another glass of lemonade
And then no more I say!

Perhaps just one banana
And one more lollipop
A little slice of Eccles cake
And then I'll *have* to stop!

So now one more one more Goodbye!
and one more slice of ham
and now goodbye forever
But first some bread and jam

So now I die, goodbye again
But pass the Stilton cheese
And as I slowly pass away
Just one more dinner please.

Spike Milligan

Jack-in-the-box

A Jack-in-the-Box
On the pantry shelf
Fell in the coffee
And hurt himself.
Nobody looked
To see what had happened:
There by the steaming
Hot urn he lay;
So they picked him up
With the silverware
And carried him off
On the breakfast tray.

William Jay Smith

The old lady of Rye

There was an old lady of Rye
Who was baked by mistake in a pie,
    To the household's disgust
    She emerged through the crust,
And exclaimed, with a yawn, 'Where am I?'

anon.

Mollie Haggarty

Poor old Mollie Haggarty
Ate chops when they were maggoty.
Now her conscience can't decide—
Did she commit insecticide?

Dorothy Barnham

The young lad of St Just

There was a young lad of St Just
Who ate apple pie till he bust.
    It wasn't the fru-it
    That caused him to do it,
What finished him off was the crust.

anon.

The old man of Peru

There was an old man of Peru,
Who dreamt he was eating his shoe.
    He woke in the night
    In a terrible fright,
And found it was perfectly true.

anon.

Lew

I don't wish to harp about Lew
Who kept peering into the stew.
    He lifted the lid
    And in it he slid.
I think I'll miss dinner, don't you?

Max Fatchen

A stormy night

It was a stormy night
one Christmas day
as they fell awake
on the Santa Fe

Turkey, jelly
and the ship's old cook
all jumped out
of a recipe book

The jelly wobbled
the turkey gobbled
and after them both
the old cook hobbled

Gobbler gobbled
Hobbler's Wobbler.
Hobbler gobbled
Wobbler's Gobbler.

Gobbly-gobbler
gobbled Wobbly
Hobbly-hobbler
Gobbled Gobbly.

Gobble gobbled
Hobble's Wobble
Hobble gobbled
gobbled Wobble.

gobble gobble
wobble wobble
hobble gobble
wobble gobble

Michael Rosen

The story of Augustus who would not have any soup

Augustus was a chubby lad;
Fat ruddy cheeks Augustus had:
And everybody saw with joy
The plump and hearty, healthy boy.
He ate and drank as he was told,
And never let his soup get cold.
But one day, one cold winter's day,
He screamed out 'Take the soup away!
O take the nasty soup away!
I won't have any soup today.'

Next day, now look, the picture shows
How lank and lean Augustus grows!
Yet, though he feels so weak and ill,
The naughty fellow cries out still
'Not any soup for me, I say:
O take the nasty soup away!
I *won't* have any soup today.'

The third day comes: Oh what a sin!
To make himself so pale and thin.
Yet, when the soup is put on table,
He screams, as loud as he is able,
'Not any soup for me, I say:
O take the nasty soup away!
I WON'T have any soup today.'

Look at him, now the fourth day's come!
He scarcely weighs a sugar-plum;
He's like a little bit of thread,
And, on the fifth day, he was—dead!

Heinrich Hoffman

Big Gumbo

Great big gawky Gumbo Cole
Couldn't stop growing to save his soul.
Gave up eating, gave up drink,
Sat in the closet, hoped to shrink;
But he grew and grew till he burst the door,
His head went through to the upper floor,
His feet reached down to the cellar door.
He grew still more till the house came down
And Gumbo Cole stepped out on the town
And smashed it in like an old anthill!
Never stopped growing, never will.
Ten times as tall as a telephone pole,
Too big for his breeches—Gumbo Cole!

William Jay Smith

Little Dimity

Poor little pigeon-toed Dimity Drew,
The more she ate, the smaller she grew.
When some people eat, they get taller and taller;
When Dimity ate, she got smaller and smaller.
She went for a walk, and all you could see
Was a tam-o'-shanter the size of a pea,
An umbrella as big as the cross on a *t*,
And a wee pocketbook of butterfly blue.
She came to a crack one half an inch wide,
Tripped on a breadcrumb, fell inside,
And slowly disappeared from view.

William Jay Smith

The Greedy Giant

There once was a giant
So far from compliant,
    He wouldn't eat toast with his tea.
'A substance so horrid
Brings pains in my forehead,
    And aches in my toe-toes,' said he, said he,
    'And aches in my toe-toes,' said he.

They brought him a tartlet
To cheer up his heartlet,
    They brought him both jelly and jam;
But still while he gobbled,
He sighed and he sobbled,
    'You *don't* know how hungry I am, I am,
    You don't *know* how hungry I am!'

They brought him a cruller
To make him feel fuller,
    They brought him some pancakes beside,
They brought him a muffin,
On which he was stuffin',
    When all of a sudden he died, he died,
    When all of a sudden he died.

Laura E. Richards

Adelaide

Adelaide was quite dismayed;
the more she ate, the less she weighed;
the less she weighed, the more she ate,
and addled Adelaide lost weight.

She stuffed herself with meat and cheese,
potatoes, pumpkins, pies, and peas,
but standing on the scale she found
that she had shed at least a pound.

She gorged herself on breasts of veal,
on roasted fish, on pickled eel,
but on completion of this feast
her scale read—ten pounds less, at least.

Poor Adelaide, that foolish glutton,
filled herself with heaps of mutton,
but when this was finally done
the scale said—minus twenty-one.

She ate until her face turned blue—
she did not know what else to do—
but when she'd finished with her plate,
she'd lost a hundred pounds of weight.

Soon Adelaide, by all accounts,
was down to hardly half an ounce,
and yet what filled her with despair
was that her cupboard shelves were bare.

For Adelaide still wished to eat—
then spied a breadcrumb by her feet;
she swiftly plucked it off the floor,
and swallowed it, then was—no more!

Jack Prelutsky

Uncle Bungle

Uncle Bungle, now deceased,
ate a cake of baker's yeast,
then with an odd gleam in his eye
consumed a large shoe-polish pie.

His dinner done, it's sad to say,
that Uncle Bungle passed away.
Uncle Bungle, now deceased,
still shines and rises in the east.

Jack Prelutsky

Still more about Mary

Mary had a little lamb,
    A lobster and some prunes,
A glass of milk, a piece of pie,
    And then some macaroons.

It made the busy waiters grin
    To see her order so,
And when they carried Mary out,
    Her face was white as snow.

anon.

Rumbletum Rapples

Rumbletum Rapples
Consumed nothing but apples
Which he ate day in and day out.
One day his boots
Turned into roots
And his ears began to sprout.
Three branches arose
From his arms and his nose
And leaves began to appear.
Now Rumbletum Rapples
Is covered in apples,
Though they taste a trifle queer.

Michael Dugan

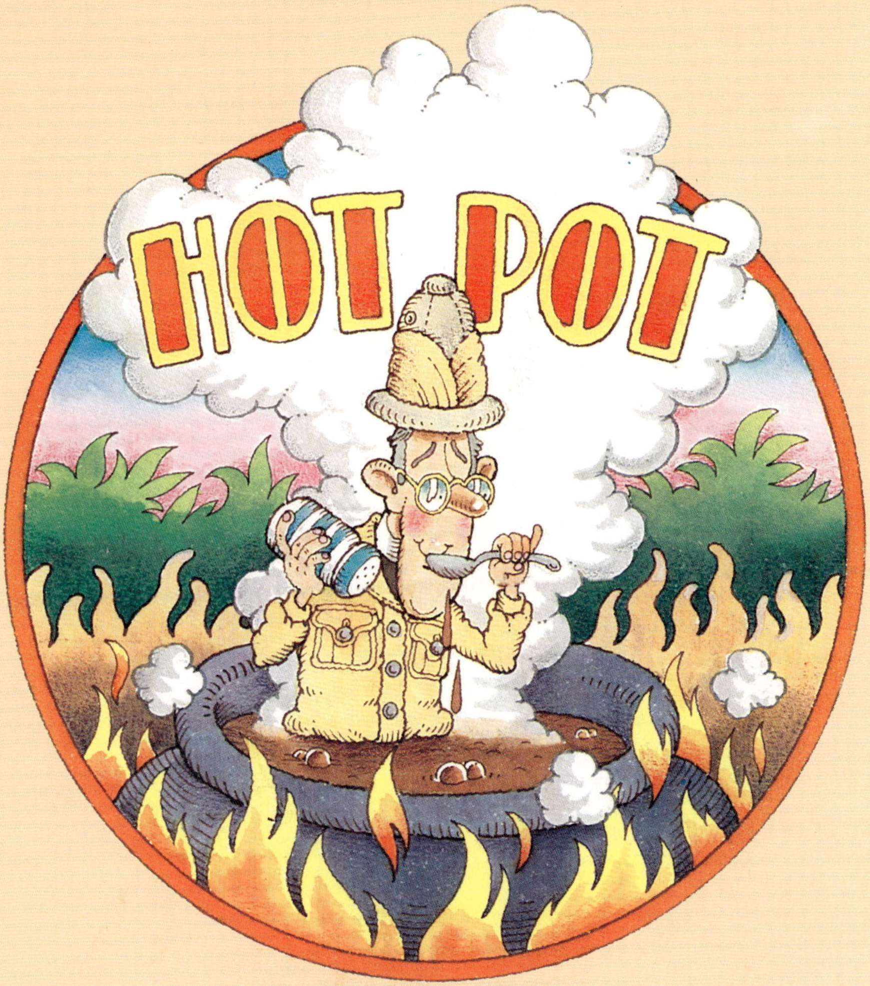
HOT POT

My Wise Old Grandpapa

When I was but a little chap
My grandpapa said to me,
'You'll need to know your manners, son
When you go out to tea.

'Remove the shells from hard-boiled eggs,
Make sure your hat's on straight,
Pour lots of honey on your peas
To keep them on the plate.

'Blow daintily upon your tea
To cool it to your taste,
And always pick bones thoroughly,
With due regard for waste.

'Be heedful of your partners' needs,
Attend their every wish;
When passing jelly, cream or jam,
Make sure they're in the dish.

'When eating figs or coconuts,
To show you are refined,
Genteely gnaw the centres out
And throw away the rind.

'If you should accidentally gulp
Some coffee while it's hot,
Just raise the lid politely and
Replace it in the pot.

'Don't butter ice cream when it's warm,
Or drink soup through a straw.'
Thus spoke my wise old grandpapa
When I was only four.

Wilbur G. Howcroft

Celery

Celery, raw,
Develops the jaw,
But celery, stewed,
Is more quietly chewed.

Ogden Nash

The greedy man

The greedy man is he who sits
And bites bits out of plates,
Or else takes up an almanac
And gobbles all the dates.

anon.

Yellow Butter

Yellow butter purple jelly red jam black bread

Spread it thick
Say it quick

Yellow butter purple jelly red jam black bread

Spread it thicker
Say it quicker

Yellow butter purple jelly red jam black bread

Now repeat it
While you eat it

Yellow butter purple jelly red jam black bread

Don't talk
With your mouth full!

Mary Ann Hoberman

A licorice stick

'Look what I have!
Look what I have!
A licorice stick!'
Said little Bess
As I walked by.

So I said,
'Can I have a bite?
I'm your friend,
Aren't I, Bess?'

And Bess just looked
And ate it all up.
And then she said, 'Yes.'

Arnold Spilka

Strange Tastes

A bad-mannered man named McDade
Ate breakfast with rake, hoe and spade.
While wearing his slippers
He liked to eat kippers
And sausage with sweet marmalade.

Marguerite Varday

Three little ghostesses

Three little ghostesses,
Sitting on postesses,
Eating buttered toastesses,
Greasing their fistesses,
Up to their wristesses.
Oh, what beastesses
To make such feastesses!

anon.

The fat lady from Skye

There was a fat lady from Skye
Who was sure she was going to die,
    But for fear that once dead
    She would not be well-fed,
She gulped down a pig, a cow, a sheep, twelve buns, a seven-
layer cake, four cups of coffee and a green apple pie.

anon.

Sneaky Bill

I'm Sneaky Bill, I'm terrible mean and vicious,
I steal all the cashews
    from the mixed-nut dishes;
I eat all the icing but I won't touch the cake,
And what you won't give me,
    I'll go ahead and take.

I gobble up the cherries from everyone's drinks,
And whenever there are sausages
    I grab a dozen links;
I take both drumsticks if
    there's turkey or chicken,
And the biggest strawberries
    are what I'm pickin';

I make sure I get the finest chop on the plate,
And I'll eat the portions of anyone who's late!

I'm always on the spot before the dinner bell—
I guess I'm pretty awful,
                    but
                  I
                      do
                          eat
                              well!

William Cole

Sammy Smith

Sammy Smith would drink and eat
    From morning until night;
He filled his mouth so full of meat,
    It was a horrid sight.

Indeed he ate and drank so fast,
    And used to stuff and cram,
The name they called him by at last
    Was Greedy, Greedy Sam.

anon.

Robin the Bobbin

Robin the Bobbin,
    the big-bellied Ben,
He ate more meat
    than fourscore men;
He ate a cow,
    he ate a calf,
He ate a butcher
    and a half,
He ate a church,
    he ate a steeple,
He ate a priest
    and all the people!
A cow and a calf,
An ox and a half,
A church and a steeple,
And all the good people,
And yet he complained
    that his stomach wasn't full.

anon.

With his mouth full of food

Milford Dupree, though he knew it was rude,
Talked with his mouth full of food.
He never would burp or walk out in the nude,
But he talked with his mouth full of food.
His mother said, 'Milford, it's crude and it's lewd
To talk with your mouth full of food.
Why, even the milk cow who moo'd as she chewed
Never moo'd with her mouth full of food.
And the cuckoo would never have ever cuckoo'd
If he coo'd with his mouth full of food.'
His dad said, 'Get married or go get tattooed,
But don't talk with your mouth full of food.
If it was a crime, you would surely get sued
If you talked with your mouth full of food.
Why, just like an animal you should be zoo'd
As you talk with your mouth full of food.
For you know we're all put in a terrible mood
When you talk with your mouth full of food.'
They pleaded and begged. He just giggled and chewed
And laughed with his mouth full of food.
And all they advised him he simply poo-poo'd,
He poo-poo'd with his mouth full of food.
So they sent for the gluer and had his mouth glued
'Cause he talked with his mouth full of food.
Now instead of 'Good morning,' he says 'Gnu murnood,
I wun tuk win mny marf furu foog.'

Shel Silverstein

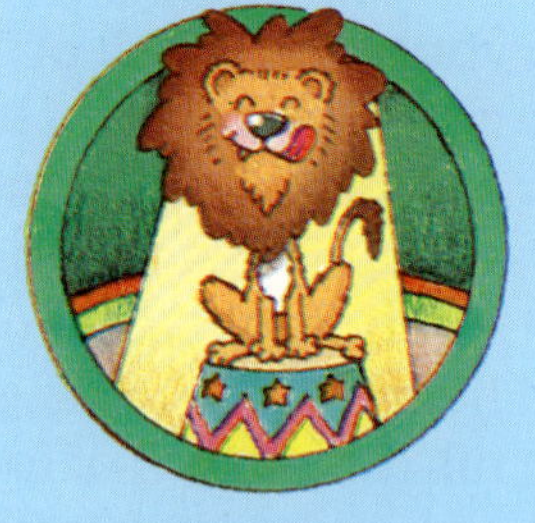

ANIMAL FARE

Said a long crocodile

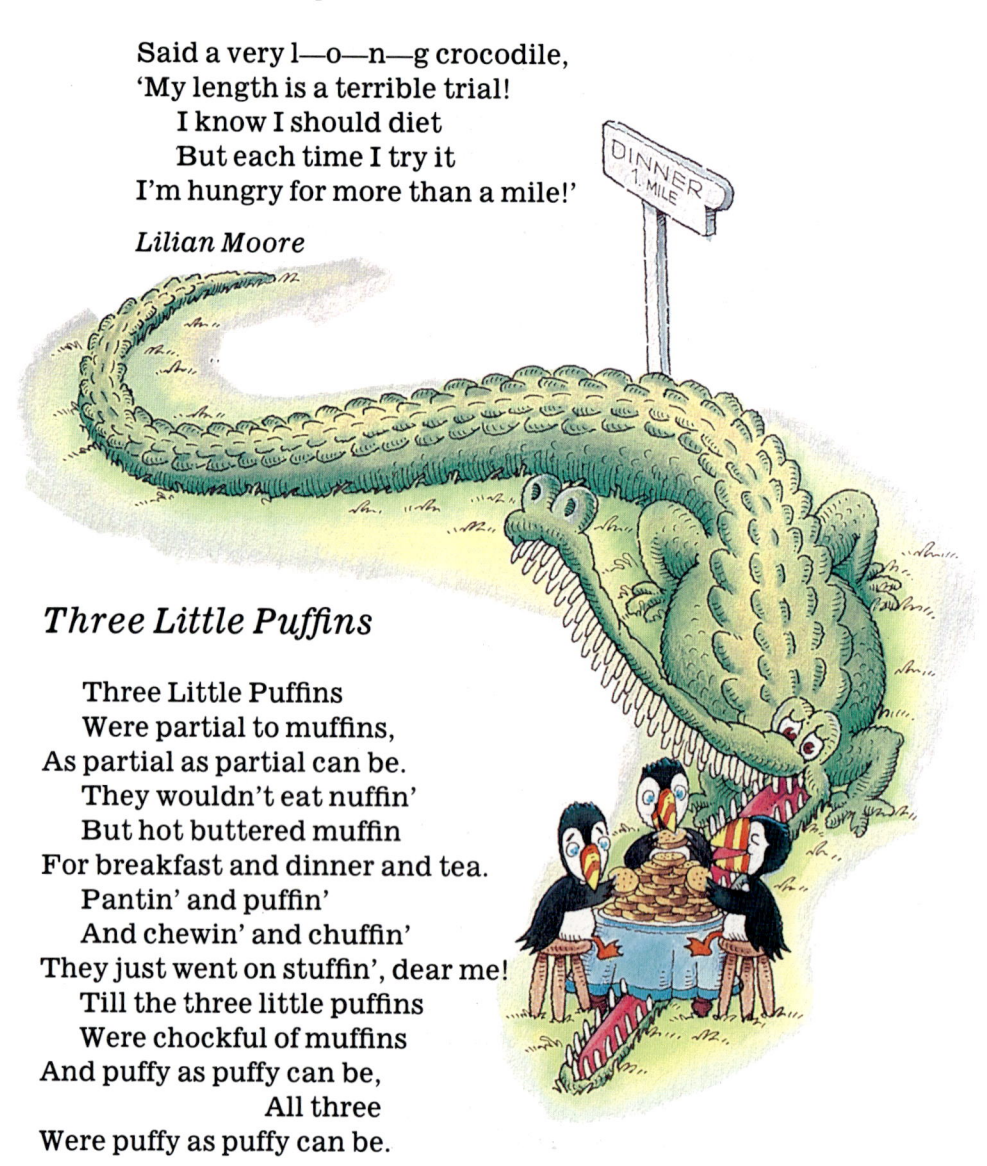

Said a very l—o—n—g crocodile,
'My length is a terrible trial!
   I know I should diet
   But each time I try it
I'm hungry for more than a mile!'

Lilian Moore

Three Little Puffins

   Three Little Puffins
   Were partial to muffins,
As partial as partial can be.
   They wouldn't eat nuffin'
   But hot buttered muffin
For breakfast and dinner and tea.
   Pantin' and puffin'
   And chewin' and chuffin'
They just went on stuffin', dear me!
   Till the three little puffins
   Were chockful of muffins
And puffy as puffy can be,
         All three
Were puffy as puffy can be.

Eleanor Farjeon

A Good Dinner

'Croak!' said the Toad, 'I'm hungry, I think;
Today I've had nothing to eat or to drink;
I'll crawl to a garden and jump through the pales,
And there I'll dine nicely on slugs and on snails.'

'Ho Ho!' quoth the Frog, 'is that what you mean?
Then I'll hop away to the next meadow stream;
There I will drink, and eat worms and slugs too,
And then I shall have a good dinner like you.'

anon.

The Leopard

The leopard always seems to feel
That he is ready for a meal,

Although he mostly comes by night
To satisfy his appetite.

And you will quickly guess, I think,
The things he likes to eat and drink.

He really is a dreadful trial,
He never takes the least denial.

And if you're out when he should call,
He waits for hours in the hall.

He is a very hungry beast,
And always ready for a feast.

Lord Alfred Douglas

Mouse Dinner

A mouse doesn't dine
on potatoes and beef...
he nibbles the seeds
from a pod or a sheaf.

He catches a beetle
and then gives a brief
little wipe of his mouth
on a napkin of leaf.

Aileen Fisher

The budgie's new year message

Get a little tin of bird-seed,
Pour it in my little trough.
If you don't, you little twit, I'll
Bite your little finger off!

Kit Wright

A hungry shark

A hungry shark some bathers eyed,
   His wife said in the spray,
'How would you like your food, my dear,
   Eat here or takeaway?'

Max Fatchen

Our Kitten

Our kitten, the one we call Louie,
Will never eat liver so chewy,
   Nor the milk, nor the fish
   That we put in his dish.
He only will dine on chop suey.

anon.

The Vulture

The vulture eats between his meals,
   And that's the reason why
He very, very rarely feels
   As well as you or I.

His eye is dull, his head is bald,
   His neck is growing thinner,
Oh! What a lesson for us all
   To only eat at dinner!

Hilaire Belloc

A fox came into my garden

A fox came into my garden.
'What do you want from me?'
'Heigh-ho, Johnnie-boy,
A chicken for my tea.'

'Oh no, you beggar, and never, you thief,
My chicken you must leave,
That she may run and she may fly
From now to Christmas Eve.'

'What are you eating, Johnnie-boy,
Between two slices of bread?'
'I'm eating a piece of chicken-breast
And it's honey-sweet,' I said.

'Heigh-ho, you diddling man,
I thought that was what I could smell.
What, some for you and none for me?
Give us a piece as well!'

Charles Causley

Whale Food

A whale liked to eat portions double.
Nothing he ate gave him trouble.
    But he just couldn't cope
    With *two* bars of soap.
And he now blows a whale of a bubble.

Lilian Moore

Beg your pardon

Some rabbits came over from Arden
And gobbled up most of my garden.
    They feasted for hours
    On stalks and on flowers
And never once said, 'Beg your pardon.'

anon.

Not-so-hot-dog

My doggie stole a sausage
And ran it down the street,
Discovered it was two-thirds bread
And only one-third meat.

So much bread in sausages
Is against the law.
Even tho' it's stolen,
The quality's still poor!

That sausage will not worry,
He knows 'twould be in vain,
For when that doggie's had one bite
He'll run it back again!

And so the English sausage
Was saved from mutilation.
That sausage lived till a hundred and nine
But the dog died of starvation.

Spike Milligan

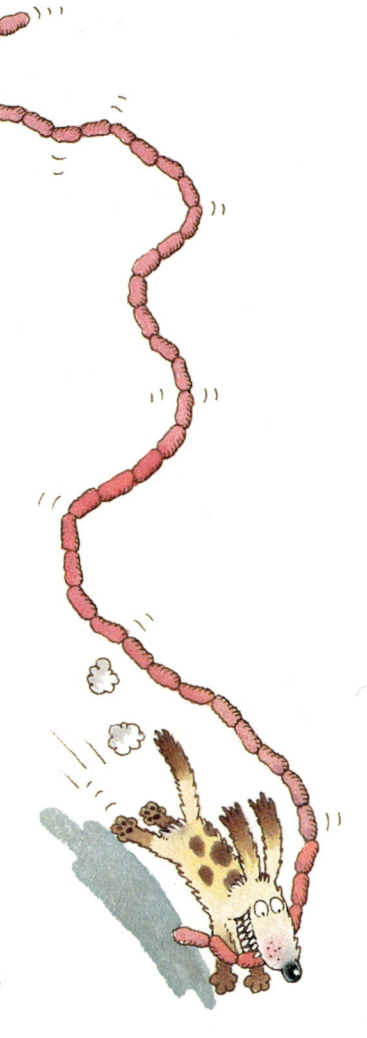

LEFTOVERS

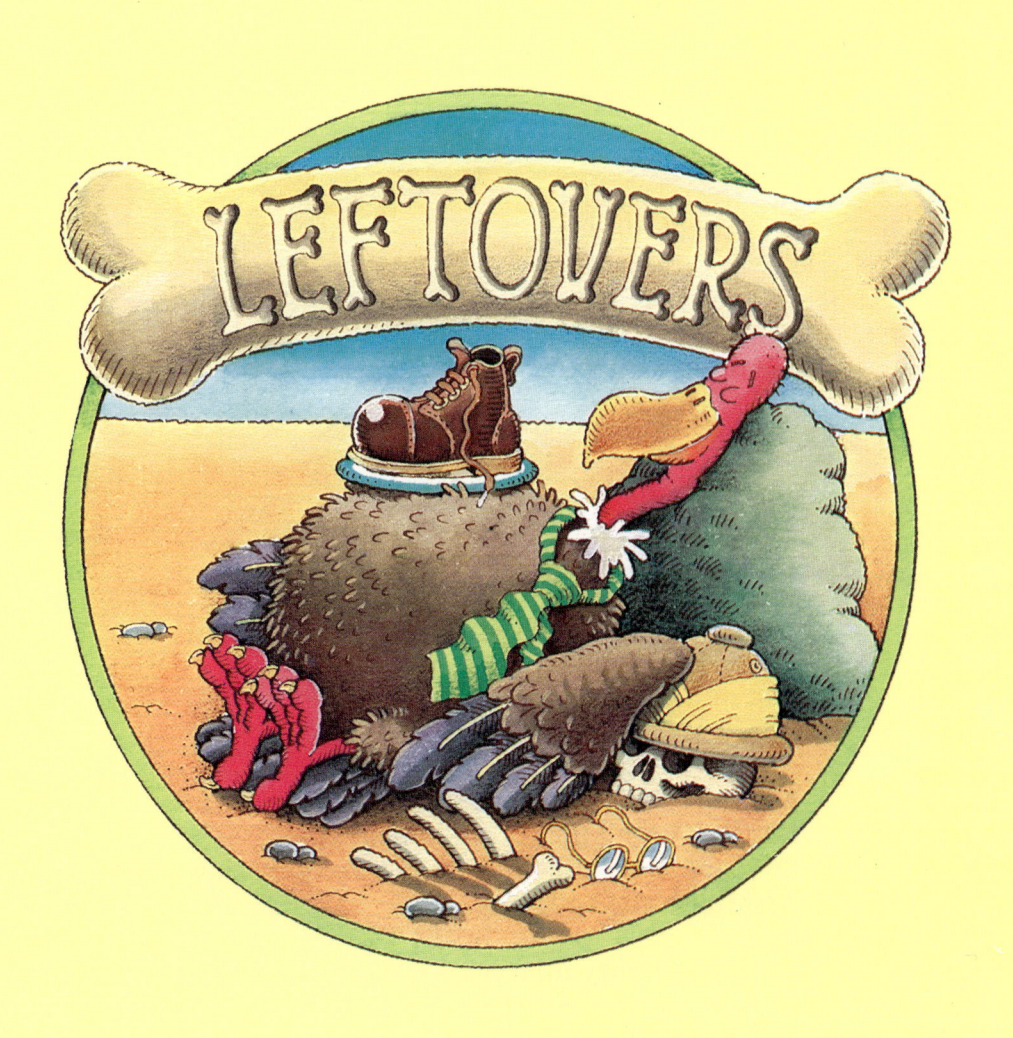

The Queen of Hearts

    The Queen of Hearts
    She made some tarts,
All on a summer's day;
    The Knave of Hearts
    He stole those tarts,
And took them clean away.

    The King of Hearts
    Called for the tarts,
And beat the knave full sore;
    The Knave of Hearts
    Brought back the tarts,
And vowed he'd steal no more.

anon.

Melinda Mae

Have you heard of tiny Melinda Mae,
Who ate a monstrous whale?
She thought she could,
She said she would,
So she started in right at the tail.

And everyone said, 'You're much too small,'
But that didn't bother Melinda at all.
She took little bites and she chewed very slow,
Just like a good girl should...

...And in eighty-nine years she ate that whale
    Because she said she would!

Shel Silverstein

Sink Song

Scouring out the porridge pot,
    Round and round and round!

Out with all the scraith and scoopery,
Lift the eely ooly droopery,
Chase the glubbery slubbery gloopery,
    Round and round and round!

Out with all the doleful dithery,
Ladle out the slimy slithery,
Hunt and catch the hithery thithery,
    Round and round and round!

Out with all the obbly gubbly,
On the stove it burns so bubbly,
Use the spoon and use it doubly,
    Round and round and round!

J. A. Lindon

Monument

A person—
a lady—
told me,
'Always ripen
peaches
in a paper bag.'
I think of her
every time
I eat one.
All summer.
Every year.

Felice Holman

Jamboree

A rhyme for ham? *Jam.*
A rhyme for mustard? *Custard.*
A rhyme for steak? *Cake.*
A rhyme for rice? *Another slice.*
A rhyme for stew? *You.*
A rhyme for mush? *Hush!*
A rhyme for prunes? *Goons.*
A rhyme for pie? *I.*
A rhyme for iced tea? *Me.*
For the pantry shelf? *Myself.*

David McCord

Thanksgiving

I feel so stuffed inside my skin
And full of little groans,
I know just how the turkey felt
Before it turned to bones.

Margaret Hillert

The Pasty

Deedle deedle dumpling, my son John,
Ate a pasty five feet long;
He bit it once, he bit it twice,
Oh, my goodness, it was full of mice!

anon.

Ask no questions

Ask no questions
tell no lies.
Ever seen mincemeat
in mince pies?

Michael Rosen

If

If all the land were apple-pie,
    And all the sea were ink;
    And all the trees were bread and cheese,
What should we do for drink?

anon.

Puddin' Proverbs

'Onions, bunions, corns and crabs,
Whiskers, wheels and hansom cabs,
Beef and bottles, beer and bones,
Give him a feed and end his groans.'

  'Eat away, chew away, munch and bolt and guzzle,
Never leave the table till you're full up to the muzzle.'

  'Politeness be sugared, politeness be hanged,
Politeness be jumbled and tumbled and banged.
  It's simply a matter of putting on pace,
Politeness has nothing to do with the case.'

Norman Lindsay

Hannah Bantry

Hannah Bantry,
In the pantry,
Gnawing at a mutton bone;
How she gnawed it,
How she clawed it,
When she found herself alone.

anon.

Giant Thunder

Giant Thunder, striding home,
Wonders if his supper's done.

'Hag wife, hag wife, bring me my bones!'
'They are not done,' the old hag moans.

'Not done? not done?' the giant roars
And heaves his old wife out of doors.

Cries he, 'I'll have them, cooked or not!'
But overturns the cooking-pot.

He flings the burning coals about;
See how the lightning flashes out!

Upon the gale the old hag rides,
The cloudy moon for terror hides.

All the world with thunder quakes;
Forest shudders, mountain shakes;
From the cloud the rainstorm breaks;
Village ponds are turned to lakes;
Every living creature wakes.

Hungry Giant, lie you still!
Stamp no more from hill to hill—
Tomorrow you shall have your fill.

James Reeves

Sweet Song

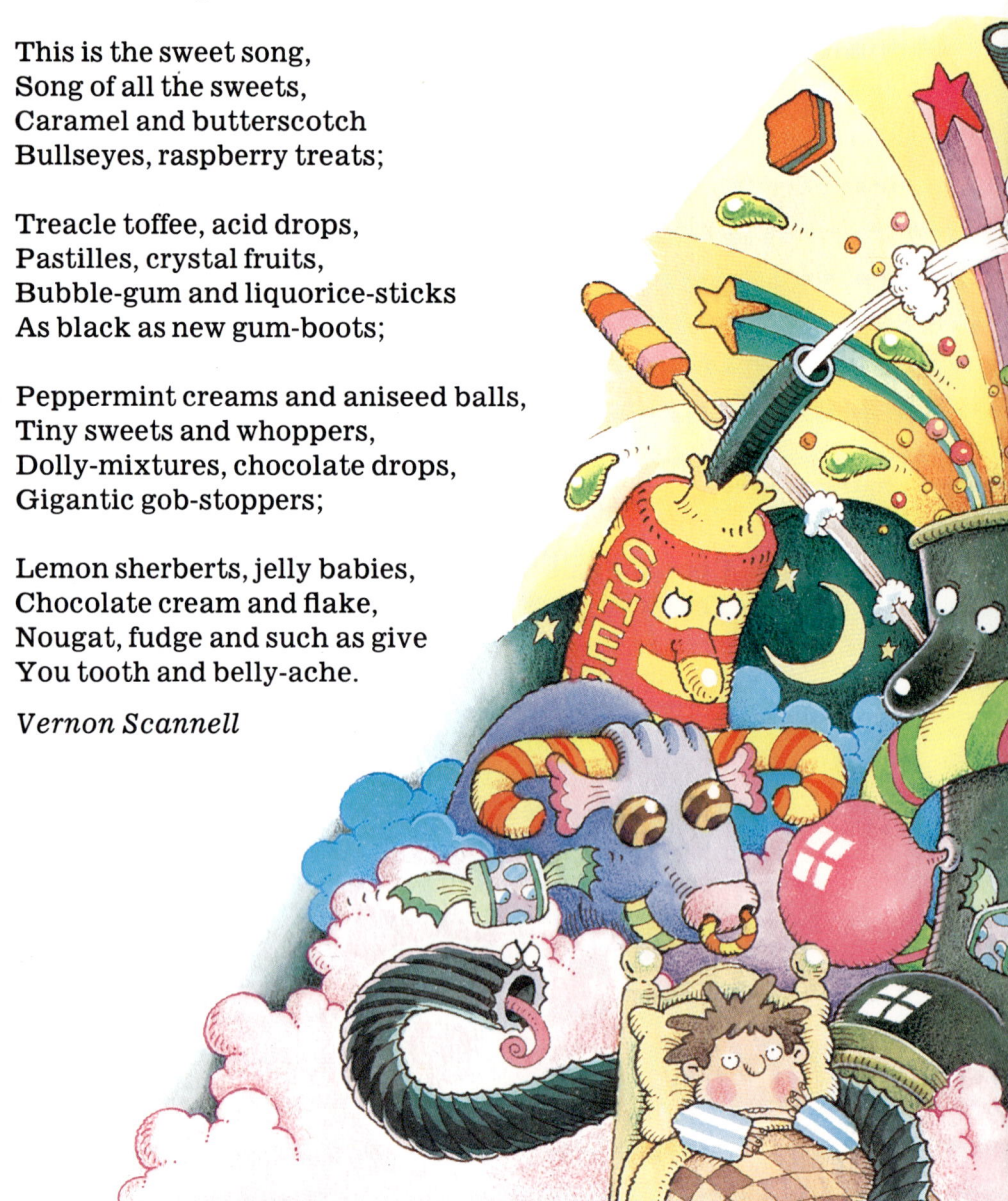

This is the sweet song,
Song of all the sweets,
Caramel and butterscotch
Bullseyes, raspberry treats;

Treacle toffee, acid drops,
Pastilles, crystal fruits,
Bubble-gum and liquorice-sticks
As black as new gum-boots;

Peppermint creams and aniseed balls,
Tiny sweets and whoppers,
Dolly-mixtures, chocolate drops,
Gigantic gob-stoppers;

Lemon sherberts, jelly babies,
Chocolate cream and flake,
Nougat, fudge and such as give
You tooth and belly-ache.

Vernon Scannell

THE END

Acknowledgements

The editor and publisher gratefully acknowledge permission to reprint the following copyright poems:

Brian Alderson: 'Lentils' from *Off and Away*, adapted by Brian Alderson. Reprinted by permission of J. M. Dent & Sons Ltd. **Dorothy Barnham:** 'Mollie Haggerty', in *More Stuff and Nonsense* (ed. Michael Dugan). **Hilaire Belloc:** 'The Vulture' from *Cautionary Verses*. Reprinted by permission of Gerald Duckworth & Co., Ltd. **Charles Causley:** 'A Fox came into my garden' from *Figgie Hobbin* (Macmillan). Reprinted by permission of David Higham Associates Ltd. **Nancy Chambers:** 'Zanzibar Pete and Zoom Along Dick' from *Stickleback, Stickleback* (Kestrel Books, 1977). Copyright © Nancy Chambers 1977. Reprinted by permission of Penguin Books Ltd. **John Ciardi:** 'Thanks anyhow' from *Fast and Slow*, Copyright © 1975 by John Ciardi. 'The Other Day When I Met Dick' and 'I Met a Man That Showed Me a Trick' from *I Met a Man*, Copyright © 1961 by John Ciardi. Reprinted by permission of Houghton Mifflin Company. **William Cole:** 'My Uncle Roasted a Kangaroo' from *Rhyme Giggles, Nonsense Giggles* (Bodley Head Ltd.,) and also in *Book of Giggles* (World Publ.). Reprinted by permission of Laurence Pollinger Ltd., and of Philomel Books (A Division of the Putnam Publ. Group). 'Sneaky Bill' from *A Boy Named Mary Jane* (Franklin Watts, 1977). Copyright © 1977 William Cole. Reprinted by permission of the author. **Charles Connell:** 'A Fisherman living in Deal ...' from *Versicles and Limericks*. Reprinted by permission of the Hamlyn Publishing Group Ltd. **Walter de la Mare:** 'The Cupboard' from *Peacock Pie* (Faber). Reprinted by permission of The Literary Trustees of Walter de la Mare and The Society of Authors as their representative. **Lord Alfred Douglas:** 'The Leopard' from *Tails With a Twist*. Copyright Edward Coleman, Executor of Lord Douglas's Literary Estate. Reprinted by permission of B. T. Batsford Limited. **Michael Dugan:** 'Obsequious Prawn' from *Stuff and Nonsense*. 'Advice to Young Cooks' and 'Rumbletum Rapples' from *More Stuff and Nonsense*. Reprinted by permission of the author. **Eleanor Farjeon:** 'V is for Vegetables' from *Invitation to a Mouse* (Pelham); 'Pimlico' from *Nursery Rhymes from London Town* (Duckworth); 'Breakfast' from *Over the Garden Wall* (Frederick Stokes); 'Minnie' from *The Children's Bells* (OUP); 'Three Little Puffins' from *Silver Sand and Snow* (Michael Joseph). All reprinted by permission of David Higham Associates Limited. **Max Fatchen:** 'Be Nice to Rhubarb'; 'A Blackberry picker called Sam'; 'I don't wish to harp about Lew' and 'A hungry shark some bathers eyed', from Max Fatchen: *Songs for my dog and other people* (Kestrel Books, 1980) pp. 58, 46, 39. Copyright © 1980 by Max Fatchen. Reprinted by permission of Penguin Books Ltd. **Aileen Fisher:** 'Mouse Dinner' from *Out in the Dark and Daylight*. Text copyright © 1980 by Aileen Fisher. Reprinted by permission of Harper & Row, Publishers, Inc. **Roy Fuller:** 'Dinner at Blunderbore's' from *Poor Roy* (1977). Reprinted by permission of Andre Deutsch Limited. **Barbara Giles:** 'Ruptured recipes' from *Stuff and Nonsense* (ed. Michael Dugan). Reprinted by permission of the author. **Mary Ann Hoberman:** 'Yellow butter' was first published in *Cricket Magazine* (Open Court Publ. Co.). Copyright © 1978 by Mary Ann Hoberman. Reprinted by permission of Harriet Wasserman Literary Agency for the author. **Felice Holman:** 'The Outlaw' and 'An Emergency' from *At the Top of My Voice*. Copyright © 1970 by Felice Holman (New York: Charles Scribner's Sons, 1970). Reprinted by permission of Charles Scribner's Sons. **Wilbur Howcroft:** 'My Wise old Grandpapa'. Reprinted by permission of the author. **James Kirkup:** 'Baby's drinking song' from *White Shadow, Black Shadow* (Dent). Reprinted by permission of Dr. Jan Van Loewen Ltd. **Steven Kroll:** 'Giant's Delight'. Copyright © 1978 by Steven Kroll. Reprinted by permission of Joan Daves. **Karla Kuskin:** 'The Meal' from *Dogs and Dragons Trees & Dreams*, Copyright © 1980 by Karla Kuskin. 'Catherine' from *In the Middle of the Trees*, Copyright © 1958 by Karla Kuskin. Reprinted by permission of Harper & Row Publishers, Inc. **J. A. Lindon:** 'Sink song'. Reprinted by permission of Hazel Lindon. **Norman Lindsay:** 'Puddin' Proverbs' from *The Magic Pudding*. Reprinted by permission of Angus & Robertson (U.K.) Ltd.

Myra Cohn Livingston: 'O sliver of liver' from *O Sliver of Liver and Other Poems*, Copyright © 1979 by Myra Cohn Livingston (New York: Atheneum, 1979). Reprinted by permission of Atheneum Publishers. **David McCord:** 'Isabel Jones and Curabel Lee', Copyright 1952 by David McCord; 'Jim', Copyright © 1967 by David McCord, both from *Mr. Bidery's Spidery Garden* (Harrap) and also in *One at a Time* (Little, Brown). Reprinted by permission of Harrap Limited and Little, Brown & Company. 'Bananas and Cream', Copyright © 1961 by David McCord; 'Cucumbers vs. pickles', Copyright © 1974 by David McCord; 'Eating at the restaurant of How Chow Now', Copyright © 1970 by David McCord; 'Jamboree', Copyright © 1965 by David McCord, all from *One at a Time*. Reprinted by permission of Little, Brown & Company. **Eve Merriam:** 'A Matter of Taste' from *There is no Rhyme for Silver* (Atheneum) Copyright © 1962 by Eve Merriam, and 'Peculiar' from *Catch a Little Rhyme* (Atheneum), Copyright © 1966 by Eve Merriam. Reprinted by permission of the author. **A. A. Milne:** 'The King's Breakfast' from *When We Were Very Young* (Methuen, 1924). Reprinted by permission of the copyright owner Mr. C. R. Milne, and Associated Book Publishers Ltd. **Cynthia Mitchell:** 'A Quick Skip Before Dinner' from *'Halloweena Hecate'* (1978). Reprinted by permission of William Heinemann Ltd. **Lilian Moore:** 'Whale food' from *See My Lovely Poison Ivy* (New York: Atheneum, 1975), Copyright © 1975 by Lilian Moore. Reprinted by permission of Atheneum Publishers. **Ogden Nash:** 'The Parsnip'; 'The Pizza', and 'The Celery' from *Custard & Co.*, and also in *Verses From 1929 On*. 'The Parsnip' and 'The Celery' are copyright 1941 by The Curtis Publishing Company and first appeared in *The Saturday Evening Post*. 'The Pizza' is copyright 1957 by Ogden Nash. Reprinted by permission of Curtis Brown Ltd. (London), on behalf of the Estate of Ogden Nash, and of Little, Brown & Company. **Sonia Nikolay:** 'Witches' Menu'. Reprinted by permission of the author. **Jack Prelutsky:** 'Pumberly Pott's Unpredictable Niece'; 'Gretchen in the Kitchen'; 'Herbert Glerbett'; 'Adelaide' and 'Uncle Bungle', all from *The Queen of Eene* by Jack Prelutsky, Copyright © 1970, 1978 by Jack Prelutsky. Reprinted by permission of Greenwillow Books (A Division of William Morrow & Co.). **James Reeves:** 'Giant Thunder' from *The Blackbird in the Lilac* (1952). Reprinted by permission of Oxford University Press. **Laura E. Richards:** 'The Greedy Giant' from *Tirra Lirra: Rhymes Old and New* Copyright 1932 by Laura E. Richards, © renewed 1960 by Hamilton Richards. Reprinted by permission of Little, Brown and Co. **Michael Rosen:** 'A Stormy Night' from *Mind Your Own Business* (1974). 'Ask no questions' from *Wouldn't You Like to Know* (1977). Reprinted by permission of Andre Deutsch Ltd. 'Uckg' is specially written for this anthology, Copyright 1982 Michael Rosen. Reprinted by permission of the author. **Vernon Scannell:** 'Special today' and 'Sweet song'. Reprinted by permission of the author. **Maurice Sendak:** 'July' from *Chicken Soup with Rice*, Copyright © 1962 by Maurice Sendak. Reprinted by permission of Harper & Row, Publishers Inc., and Collins Publishers (Nutshell Library). **Shel Silverstein:** 'With his mouth full of food'; 'Hungry Mungry' and 'Melinda Mae' from *Where the Sidewalk Ends*, Copyright 1974 by Shel Silverstein. Reprinted by permission of Harper & Row Publishers Inc. **William Jay Smith:** 'Big Gumbo'; 'Little Dimity' and 'Jack-in-the-box' from *Laughing Time: Nonsense Poems* by William Jay Smith (Delacorte Press, 1980), Copyright © 1953, 1955, 1956, 1957, 1959, 1968, 1974, 1977, 1980 by William Jay Smith. Reprinted by permission of the author and Delacorte Press/Seymour Lawrence. **Arnold Spilka:** 'Karen doesn't like a cone...' and 'A Liquorice stick' from *A Rumbudgin of Nonsense* (Scribners 1970), Copyright © 1970 Arnold Spilka. Reprinted by permission of Frances Schwartz Literary Agency. **Marguerite Varday:** 'Strange tastes' from *More Stuff and Nonsense* (ed. Michael Dugan). Reprinted by permission of the author. **Clyde Watson:** 'Dilly Dilly Piccalilli' from *Father Foxes Pennyrhymes*. Text copyright © 1971 by Clyde Watson. Reprinted by permission of Macmillan, London and Basingstoke and of Thomas Y. Crowell, Publisher. **Kit Wright:** 'The Fate of the Supermarket Manager'; 'Say Cheese'; 'If You're no good at cooking' and 'Give up slimming Mum', from *Rabbiting On*. Reprinted by permission of Fontana Paperbacks. 'Dave Dirt Came To Dinner'; and 'The Budgie's New Year Message' from *Hot Dog & Other Poems* (Kestrel Books, 1981) pp. 61, 35. Text copyright © 1981 Kit Wright. Reprinted by permission of Penguin Books Ltd.

Although every effort has been made to trace and contact copyright holders, this has not always been possible. If they contact the Publisher, correct acknowledgement will be made in future editions.

Index of Titles and First Lines

A bad-mannered man named McDade 85
A hungry shark some bathers eyed 94
A Jack-in-the-box 68
A mouse doesn't dine 94
A peanut sat on the railroad track 38
A person 101
A rhyme for ham? Jam 102
A whale liked to eat portions double 96
Adelaide 75
Adelaide was quite dismayed 75
Advice to young cooks 47
An Emergency 50
Ask no questions 103
At Christmas the STILTON 25
Augustus was a chubby lad 71

Baby's Drinking Song 53
Bananas and cream 26
Beautiful Soup 31
Beautiful Soup, so rich and green 31
Before you start to cook 47
Beg your pardon 97
Be nice to rhubarb 24
Betty Botter's batter 39
Betty Botter bought some butter 39
Blackberry Picker called Sam, A 31
Big Gumbo 72
Breakfast 51
Budgie's New Year Message, The 94

Catherine 42
Catherine said, 'I think I'll bake' 42
Celery 83
Celery, raw 83
Chicken and Chips 22
Cinnamon and arrowroot 44
Cries of London 8
'Croak!' said the Toad, 'I'm hungry, I think' 93
Cupboard, The 11

Cucumbers always give me squirms 29
Cucumbers vs. Pickles 29

Dave Dirt came to Dinner 55
Davy Davy Dumpling 43
Davy Dumpling 43
Deedle deedle dumpling, my son John 102
Dilly Dilly Picalilli 29
Dinner at Blunderbore's 56

Eating at the Restaurant of How Chow Now 60
Ever eaten Chinese food? 60

Fat lady from Skye, The 86
Fate of the Supermarket Manager, The 17
Fee, fi, fo, fum 57
Fisherman living in Deal, A 20
Fox came into my garden, A 96

Get a little tin of bird-seed 94
Giant, The 57
Giant's Delight 23
Giant Thunder 105
Giant Thunder, striding home 105
Give up slimming, Mum 58
Glutton, The 67
Good Dinner, A 93
Great big gawky Gumbo Cole 72
Greedy Giant, The 74
Greedy Man, The 83
Gretchen in the Kitchen 37

Hannah Bantry 104
Have you heard of tiny Melinda Mae 100
Herbert Glerbett 66
Herbert Glerbett, rather round 66
Here are fine golden pippins 8
Here are some of our favourite foods 22

110

Here's round and sound 8
Hot cross buns, hot cross buns 8
Hungry Mungry 78
Hungry Mungry sat at supper 78
Hungry Shark, A 94

I don't wish to harp about Lew 69
I feel so stuffed inside my skin 102
I know a little cupboard 11
I met a man that showed me a trick 62
I once knew a boy who was odd as could be 27
I see you're here to sneak some looks 37
If 103
If all the land were apple-pie 103
If you stay to school dinners 53
If you're no good at cooking 43
I'm 6
I'm Sneaky Bill, I'm terrible mean and vicious 87
In July 12
Into the house of Mrs MacGruder 12
Is it coffee for breakfast? 51
Isabel Jones & Curabel Lee 21
It was a stormy night 70

Jack-in-the-box 68
Jam 52
Jamboree 102
July 12

Karen doesn't like a cone 21
King Arthur 40
King's Breakfast, The 14
Lentils 38
Lentils, lentils 38
Leopard, The 93
Lew 69
Licorice Stick, A 85
Little Dimity 73
Little Miss Muffet 61
Live lizard, dead lizard 46
Look at itsy-bitsy Mitzi 28
Look what I have 85

Mary had a little lamb (1) 54
Mary had a little lamb (2) 76

Matter of Taste, A 20
Meal, The 28
Melinda Mae 100
Milford, Dupree, though he knew it was rude 89
Minnie 57
Minnie can't make her mind up 57
Mollie Haggarty 68
Monument 101
Mouse dinner 94
My doggie stole a sausage 97
My mum 58
My uncle roasted a Kangaroo 30
My wise old grandpapa 82

Not-so-hot-dog 97

O Sliver of Liver 27
Obsequious Prawn 11
Oh Molly, Molly, Molly 67
Old lady of Rye, The 68
Old man of Peru, The 69
Old woman of Ryde, The 79
One summer at tea 63
Once I went to the fridge 40
Onions, bunions, corns and crabs 104
Our kitten 95
Our kitten the one we call Louie 95
Outlaw, The 12

Parsnip, The 27
Pasty, The 102
Peanut, A 38
Peanut Seller, The 10
Peanuts! 10
Pears for pies 9
Peculiar 27
Peepy pipey peppercorn 39
Picnic, The 62
Pimlico 38
Pimlico, pamlico, pumpkins and peas! 38
Pizza, The 28
Please say a word for rhubarb 24
Poor little pigeon toed Dimity Drew 73
Poor old Molly Haggarty 68
Puddin' proverbs 104

Pumberley Pott's unpredictable niece 32

Queen of Hearts, The 100
Quick skip before dinner, A 39
Rain, frost, or snow, hot or cold 9
Robbin the Bobbin 88
Rumpleton Rapples 77
Ruptured Recipes 44

Said a long crocodile 92
Said a very l—o—n—g crocodile 92
Salt, mustard, vinegar, pepper 63
Sammy Smith 88
Sammy Smith would drink and eat 88
Say Cheese 25
School dinners 53
Scouring out the porridge pot 101
Sink song 101
Sip a little 53
Sneaky Bill 87
Some rabbit came over from Arden 97
Special Today 36
'Spread' said toast to butter 52
Still more about Mary 76
Stormy Night, A 70
Story of Augustus who would not have any soup, The 71
Strange Tastes 85
Sunday morning 50
Supermarket 6
Sweet song 106

Taffy was a Welshman 13
Thanks anyhow 30
Thanksgiving 102
The country vegetables scorn 10
The giant Blunderbore 56
The greedy man is he who sits 83
The King asked 14
The leopard always seems to feel 93
The other day when I met Dick 54
The parsnip, children, I repeat 27
The vulture eats between his meals 95
There once was a giant 74

There once was a Supermarket manager 17
There was a fat lady from Skye 86
There was a King 51
There was a King who had four sons 51
There was a young lad of St Just 69
There was a young parson named Perkins 63
There was an old lady of Rye 68
There was an old man of Peru 69
There was an old woman of Ryde 79
This is the sweet song 106
Timothy Tompkins had turnips and tea 28
Three Little Puffins 92
Three Little ghostesses 86
Through the teeth 50

UCKG! 40
Uncle Bungle 76
Uncle Bungle now deceased 76

Vats of soup 23
V is for vegetables 10
Vulture, The 95

We brought a rug for sitting on 62
We can recommend our soups 36
Witches' Menu 46
Whale food 96
What does your tongue like the most? 20
What's in the cupboard? 46
When good King Arthur ruled this land 40
When I was a boy in your town 30
When I was but a little chap 82
With his mouth full of food 89

Yellow butter 84
Yellow butter, purple jelly, red jam 84
Young lad of St Just, The 69

Zanzibar Pete and Zoom-along Dick 52